$9 \times 9 = ?$

$476 + 322 = ?$

$8 \times 12 = ?$

$34 \times 67 = ?$

$5/6 \div 1/2 = ?$

$3.5 \div 7 = ?$

$298 \times 6 = ?$

$77 \div 6 = ?$

2019 Catherine Fet, Leonid Erostanetsky
North Landing Books
all rights reserved

YES, IT LOOKS SCARY!

AS YOU HOLD THIS BOOK IN YOUR HANDS,
I KNOW WHAT YOU ARE THINKING:
MATH IS HARD. MATH IS NO FUN. MATH IS SCARY!

HEY, BELIEVE IT OR NOT, I AGREE WITH YOU.
WHEN I WAS A KID, I NEVER THOUGHT:
I AM SO LOOKING FORWARD TO MULTIPLYING 7×8! WOOHOO!
OR *I JUST LOVE ADDING FRACTIONS WITH DIFFERENT DENOMINATORS! CAN'T WAIT TO FIND OUT THE SUM OF $\frac{3}{9}$ PLUS $\frac{9}{8}$!*

I struggled with times tables, and hated word problems like: Helen has bought 7 boxes of 4 cupcakes each. How many cupcakes in all has Helen bought? Are you kidding me??? There I was, drowning in math and misery, and, as if my suffering was not enough, they were telling me about 7 boxes of cupcakes! I would have died for just one cupcake!...

OK, now that you know the truth about me, let me tell you how I defeated the math monster with speed math.

What is Speed Math?

Speed math is using tricks to make calculations easy. For example, can you solve these problems instantly, in your mind, without writing down anything?

357 − 280 = ?
247 x 11 = ?
1/3 + 1/5 = ?

I can. And I will show you how. It's easy if you know the trick. Tricks don't work in every situation, but if you learn just a few, they will make your life much much easier. The math monster will grow a bit friendlier!

Easy Times Tables

Memorizing times tables is a big task. There is no way around this: You must learn the times tables by heart to be good at math. You need to be able to recall instantly, without thinking, what 5 x 9 is, or 6 x 8, or 7 x 7... The good news is that there are tricks that will help you learn the times tables in no time! Think of these tricks as **MENTAL CHEAT SHEETS!**

Scary Tables

In many school math books, the times tables look like this.

Turn the page to see which of these you should start memorizing first...

Oh no, I am lost.

1 × 1 = 1	1 × 2 = 2	1 × 3 = 3	1 × 4 = 4
2 × 1 = 2	2 × 2 = 4	2 × 3 = 6	2 × 4 = 8
3 × 1 = 3	3 × 2 = 6	3 × 3 = 9	3 × 4 = 12
4 × 1 = 4	4 × 2 = 8	4 × 3 = 12	4 × 4 = 16
5 × 1 = 5	5 × 2 = 10	5 × 3 = 15	5 × 4 = 20
6 × 1 = 6	6 × 2 = 12	6 × 3 = 18	6 × 4 = 24
7 × 1 = 7	7 × 2 = 14	7 × 3 = 21	7 × 4 = 28
8 × 1 = 8	8 × 2 = 16	8 × 3 = 24	8 × 4 = 32
9 × 1 = 9	9 × 2 = 18	9 × 3 = 27	9 × 4 = 36
10 × 1 = 10	10 × 2 = 20	10 × 3 = 30	10 × 4 = 40
11 × 1 = 11	11 × 2 = 22	11 × 3 = 33	11 × 4 = 44
12 × 1 = 12	12 × 2 = 24	12 × 3 = 36	12 × 4 = 48

1 × 5 = 5	1 × 6 = 6	1 × 7 = 7	1 × 8 = 8
2 × 5 = 10	2 × 6 = 12	2 × 7 = 14	2 × 8 = 16
3 × 5 = 15	3 × 6 = 18	3 × 7 = 21	3 × 8 = 24
4 × 5 = 20	4 × 6 = 24	4 × 7 = 28	4 × 8 = 32
5 × 5 = 25	5 × 6 = 30	5 × 7 = 35	5 × 8 = 40
6 × 5 = 30	6 × 6 = 36	6 × 7 = 42	6 × 8 = 48
7 × 5 = 35	7 × 6 = 42	7 × 7 = 49	7 × 8 = 56
8 × 5 = 40	8 × 6 = 48	8 × 7 = 56	8 × 8 = 64
9 × 5 = 45	9 × 6 = 54	9 × 7 = 63	9 × 8 = 72
10 × 5 = 50	10 × 6 = 60	10 × 7 = 70	10 × 8 = 80
11 × 5 = 55	11 × 6 = 66	11 × 7 = 77	11 × 8 = 88
12 × 5 = 60	12 × 6 = 72	12 × 7 = 84	12 × 8 = 96

1 × 9 = 9	1 × 10 = 10	1 × 11 = 11	1 × 12 = 12
2 × 9 = 18	2 × 10 = 20	2 × 11 = 22	2 × 12 = 24
3 × 9 = 27	3 × 10 = 30	3 × 11 = 33	3 × 12 = 36
4 × 9 = 36	4 × 10 = 40	4 × 11 = 44	4 × 12 = 48
5 × 9 = 45	5 × 10 = 50	5 × 11 = 55	5 × 12 = 60
6 × 9 = 54	6 × 10 = 60	6 × 11 = 66	6 × 12 = 72
7 × 9 = 63	7 × 10 = 70	7 × 11 = 77	7 × 12 = 84
8 × 9 = 72	8 × 10 = 80	8 × 11 = 88	8 × 12 = 96
9 × 9 = 81	9 × 10 = 90	9 × 11 = 99	9 × 12 = 108
10 × 9 = 90	10 × 10 = 100	10 × 11 = 110	10 × 12 = 120
11 × 9 = 99	11 × 10 = 110	11 × 11 = 121	11 × 12 = 132
12 × 9 = 108	12 × 10 = 120	12 × 11 = 132	12 × 12 = 144

1 x 1 = 1	1 x 2 = 2	1 x 3 = 3	1 x 4 = 4
2 x 1 = 2	2 x 2 = 4	2 x 3 = 6	2 x 4 = 8
3 x 1 = 3	3 x 2 = 6	3 x 3 = 9	3 x 4 = 12
4 x 1 = 4	4 x 2 = 8	4 x 3 = 12	4 x 4 = 16
5 x 1 = 5	5 x 2 = 10	5 x 3 = 15	5 x 4 = 20
6 x 1 = 6	6 x 2 = 12	6 x 3 = 18	6 x 4 = 24
7 x 1 = 7	7 x 2 = 14	7 x 3 = 21	7 x 4 = 28
8 x 1 = 8	8 x 2 = 16	8 x 3 = 24	8 x 4 = 32
9 x 1 = 9	9 x 2 = 18	9 x 3 = 27	9 x 4 = 36
10 x 1 = 10	10 x 2 = 20	10 x 3 = 30	10 x 4 = 40
11 x 1 = 11	11 x 2 = 22	11 x 3 = 33	11 x 4 = 44
12 x 1 = 12	12 x 2 = 24	12 x 3 = 36	12 x 4 = 48

HAHAHA... NOT THIS ONE.   BABY STUFF, NOPE.   MEH. NOT NOW.   WHA? NAH. BABY STUFF TIMES TWO.

1 x 5 = 5	1 x 6 = 6	1 x 7 = 7	1 x 8 = 8
2 x 5 = 10	2 x 6 = 12	2 x 7 = 14	2 x 8 = 16
3 x 5 = 15	3 x 6 = 18	3 x 7 = 21	3 x 8 = 24
4 x 5 = 20	4 x 6 = 24	4 x 7 = 28	4 x 8 = 32
5 x 5 = 25	5 x 6 = 30	5 x 7 = 35	5 x 8 = 40
6 x 5 = 30	6 x 6 = 36	6 x 7 = 42	6 x 8 = 48
7 x 5 = 35	7 x 6 = 42	7 x 7 = 49	7 x 8 = 56
8 x 5 = 40	8 x 6 = 48	8 x 7 = 56	8 x 8 = 64
9 x 5 = 45	9 x 6 = 54	9 x 7 = 63	9 x 8 = 72
10 x 5 = 50	10 x 6 = 60	10 x 7 = 70	10 x 8 = 80
11 x 5 = 55	11 x 6 = 66	11 x 7 = 77	11 x 8 = 88
12 x 5 = 60	12 x 6 = 72	12 x 7 = 84	12 x 8 = 96

HMMM.... MAYBE NOT.   GIVE ME A BREAK! JUST IGNORE!

1 x 9 = 9	1 x 10 = 10	1 x 11 = 11	1 x 12 = 12
2 x 9 = 18	2 x 10 = 20	2 x 11 = 22	2 x 12 = 24
3 x 9 = 27	3 x 10 = 30	3 x 11 = 33	3 x 12 = 36
4 x 9 = 36	4 x 10 = 40	4 x 11 = 44	4 x 12 = 48
5 x 9 = 45	5 x 10 = 50	5 x 11 = 55	5 x 12 = 60
6 x 9 = 54	6 x 10 = 60	6 x 11 = 66	6 x 12 = 72
7 x 9 = 63	7 x 10 = 70	7 x 11 = 77	7 x 12 = 84
8 x 9 = 72	8 x 10 = 80	8 x 11 = 88	8 x 12 = 96
9 x 9 = 81	9 x 10 = 90	9 x 11 = 99	9 x 12 = 108
10 x 9 = 90	10 x 10 = 100	10 x 11 = 110	10 x 12 = 120
11 x 9 = 99	11 x 10 = 110	11 x 11 = 121	11 x 12 = 132
12 x 9 = 108	12 x 10 = 120	12 x 11 = 132	12 x 12 = 144

SERIOUSLY? YOU CAN DO THESE IN YOUR SLEEP!   THERE IS A TRICK FOR THIS ONE TOO.

GOOD STUFF

OK, SO HERE IS THE ONLY TIMES TABLE YOU NEED.
I HAVE COLORED THE SQUARES WORTH MEMORIZING.

(Handwritten annotations: 3×3=9, 5×8=40)

1	2	3	4	5	6	7	8	9	10	11	12
2	4	6	8	10	12	14	16	18	20	22	24
3	6	**9**	**12**	15	**18**	**21**	**24**	27	30	33	36
4	8	12	**16**	20	**24**	**28**	**32**	36	40	44	48
5	10	15	20	25	**30**	**35**	**40**	45	50	55	60
6	12	18	24	30	36	42	48	54	60	66	72
7	14	21	28	35	42	49	56	63	70	77	84
8	16	24	32	40	48	56	64	72	80	88	96
9	18	27	36	45	54	63	72	81	90	99	108
10	20	30	40	50	60	70	80	90	100	110	120
11	22	33	44	55	66	77	88	99	110	121	132
12	24	36	48	60	72	84	96	108	120	132	144

<u>ONLY 12 SQUARES!</u> IF YOU CAN LEARN THEM BY HEART TODAY OR TOMORROW, YOU CAN DO THE ENTIRE MULTIPLICATION TABLE RIGHT AWAY, BECAUSE I WILL TEACH YOU TRICKS TO MULTIPLY ALL THE OTHER NUMBERS ON THIS TABLE. THESE TRICKS ARE JUST A START. TO BE GOOD AT MATH YOU NEED TO KNOW YOUR TIMES TABLES SO WELL THAT YOU DON'T STOP TO THINK EVEN FOR A MOMENT. BUT WHEN YOU JUST START LEARNING THEM, TRICKS HELP YOU GET AHEAD FAST. THEY ARE YOUR *MENTAL CHEAT SHEETS!*

EASY STUFF

First, let's get zero out of the way.
Times 0. Any number times 0 equals 0.
Any scary number x 0 = 0 (big fat zero, zilch, nada!)

Next. Any number **times 1** is that same number.
Any scary number x 1 = that same number!!
Examples:
2 x 1 = 2
1,000,000 x 1 = 1,000,000

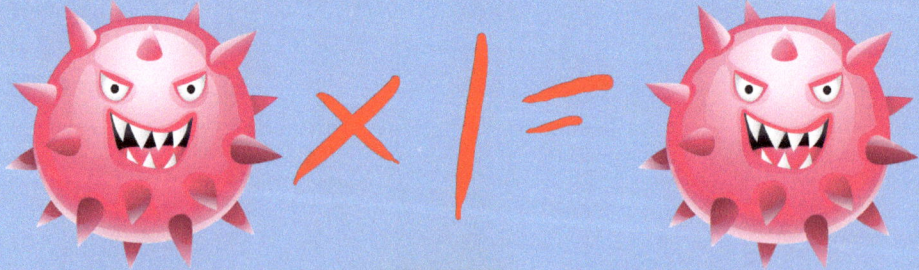

Moving on... Any number **times 2** ...
Just add that number to itself!
You learned it in kindergarten, right?
2 x 2 = 2 + 2 = 4
3 x 2 = 3 + 3 = 6
4 x 2 = 4 + 4 = 8

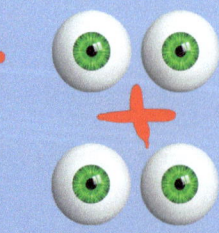

... and so on.
Yawn. Easy! Even this one:
12 x 2 = 12 + 12 = 10 + 10 + 2 + 2 = 24
Nothing to memorize so far.

SCARY BIG NUMBERS

So now you are thinking: Zero, one and two are easy. What happens when we arrive at 9, 10, 11, and 12 - ???! Admit it: You are scared of those big numbers. I was scared of them as a kid, until I learned a few secret tricks.

11 x 12 — SECRET TRICKS

Times 9. Here is our first **MENTAL CHEAT SHEET**. You can multiply x 9 on your fingers! Say you want to do 3 x 9. OK, counting from the left, bend the 3rd finger:

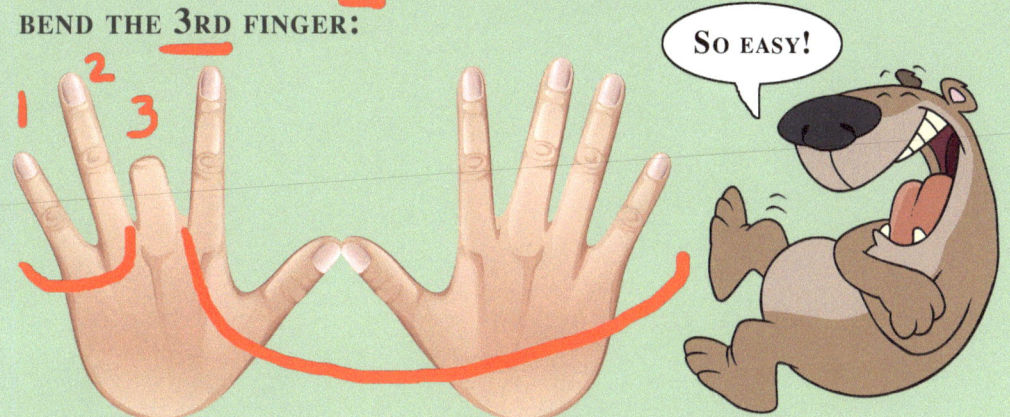

So easy!

Now count the fingers to the left of the bent finger: 2
Next count the fingers to the right of the bent finger: 7
Your answer is 27.
3 x 9 = 27 Guess what: It works for any number from 1 to 10. That's your x9 cheat sheet!

I Love x 9!

Here is another cool thing about x9.
You can write the entire x9 multiplication table
in less than 30 seconds! Write 1 through 9.
Then shift right by 1 digit and write those numbers again.

1 2 3 4 5 6 7 8 9
  1 2 3 4 5 6 7 8

Next reverse the numbers on the bottom,
and write them again below:

1 2 3 4 5 6 7 8 9
  1 2 3 4 5 6 7 8
  8 7 6 5 4 3 2 1

Look!
2 x 9 = 18   3 x 9 = 27   7 x 9 = 63   9 x 9 = 81 - !!!!!

Trust me, we'll defeat that Math Monster!

More Scary Big Numbers
(not scary anymore!)

Times 10. Just write a zero at the end of any number, and you have multiplied it by 10!

5 x 10 = 50
7 x 10 = 70
1,000,000 x 10 = 10,000,000

10 is just silly! Kick it out of your times table!

Times 11.
With any number up to 9, just write that number 2 times and you have multiplied it by 11.

2 x 11 = 22   3 x 11 = 33   9 x 11 = 99

Want to know how to do 43 x 11 instantly? You are in for a big shock! Don't fall off your chair!

You take 43, and you go like this: 4 + 3 = 7
Now put 7 between 4 and 3 - and that is your answer!
No kidding: 43 x 11 = 4 (4+3) 3 = 473
Yes, that's it.
Let's try 36 x 11.
36 x 11 = 3 (3+6) 6 = 396
Works for any number in the world!
If the sum of the numbers makes a 2-digit number, you just carry the tens digit, like when you add big numbers.
68 x 11 = 6 (6+8) 8 = 6 (14) 8 = 748
97 x 11 = 9 (9+7) 7 = 9 (16) 7 = 1067

ANY NUMBER x 9

Here is a super easy way to multiply any number x9, not just the numbers you can do on your fingers.
Let's do 14 x 9.
1. Multiply your number x10 (just add a zero!)
14 x 10 = 140
2. Take away your number from the result:
140 − 14 = 126

Because 9 is just one less than 10, when we do 14 x 10 we get 14 ten times,

14　14　14　14　14　14　14　14　14　14
 1   2   3   4   5   6   7   8   9   10   = 140

but we need it only 9 times, so take away one 14

14　14　14　14　14　14　14　14　14　~~14~~
 1   2   3   4   5   6   7   8   9   ~~10~~

140 − 14 = 126

Yesss!

x 11 Magic Trick

I CAN TEACH YOU AN AMAZING MATH MAGIC TRICK. FIRST, LEARN TO MULTIPLY 1 AND 2-DIGIT NUMBERS X 11.

MAKE A LIST LIKE THIS. GIVE IT TO A FRIEND AND ASK THEM TO WRITE ANY NUMBER BETWEEN 1 AND 20 ON LINE 1, AND ANY NUMBER BETWEEN 1 AND 20 ON LINE 2. NEXT THEY SHOULD ADD LINES 1 AND 2 AND WRITE THE RESULT ON LINE 3. THEN THEY SHOULD ADD LINES 2 AND 3 AND WRITE THE RESULT ON LINE 4, AND SO ON TO THE END OF THE LIST. IF THEY NEED A CALCULATOR, GO AHEAD AND GIVE THEM ONE!

NEXT HAVE YOUR FRIEND SHOW YOU THE LIST. THEN YOU SAY: *I CAN TELL YOU THE SUM OF ALL THE NUMBERS ON THE LIST, RIGHT NOW, WITHOUT ANY CALCULATOR.* IF THE LIST LOOKS LIKE THIS, YOU WILL SAY: *IT'S 517.* LET THEM USE THE CALCULATOR TO CHECK YOUR ANSWER, AND REALIZE TO THEIR AMAZEMENT THAT YOUR ANSWER IS CORRECT! HOW DID YOU DO IT? YOU JUST MULTIPLIED LINE 7 OF THE LIST BY 11.
47 x 11 = 4 (4+7) 7 = 517   IT'S MAGIC!

Line	Value
1	___
2	___
3	___
4	___
5	___
6	___
7	___
8	___
9	___
10	___

Line	Value
1	3
2	4
3	7
4	11
5	18
6	29
7	47
8	76
9	123
10	199

The Biggest of Them All

Times 12. Let's do 2 x 12 and learn a new trick!

2 x 12 = 2 (2x2) = 24

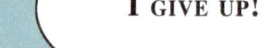

I give up!

Just copy the first number: 2
Then multiply it by 2: 2 x 2 = 4
Write them side-by-side: 24
Your answer is 24!

Here is our Times 12 table:
3 x 12 = 3 (3x2) = 36
4 x 12 = 4 (4x2) = 48

5 x 12 = 5 (5x2) = 5 (10) carry 1 = 60

6 x 12 = 6 (6x2) = 6 (12) carry 1 = 72

7 x 12 = 7 (7x2) = 7 (14) carry 1 = 84

8 x 12 = 8 (8x2) = 8 (16) carry 1 = 96

9 x 12 = 9 (9x2) = 9 (18) carry 1 = 108

10 x 12 = same as 12 x 10 = 120

11 x 12 = same as 12 x 11 = 1 (1+2)2 = 132

12 x 12 = 12 (12x2) = 12 (24) carry 2 = 144

The Times 12 monster is defeated!

Even Bigger?

I know you are going to ask me:
Does this x12 trick work with big 2-digit numbers?
Like 74 x 12 ?
Sure. But it's a bit different. So let's try 74 x 12

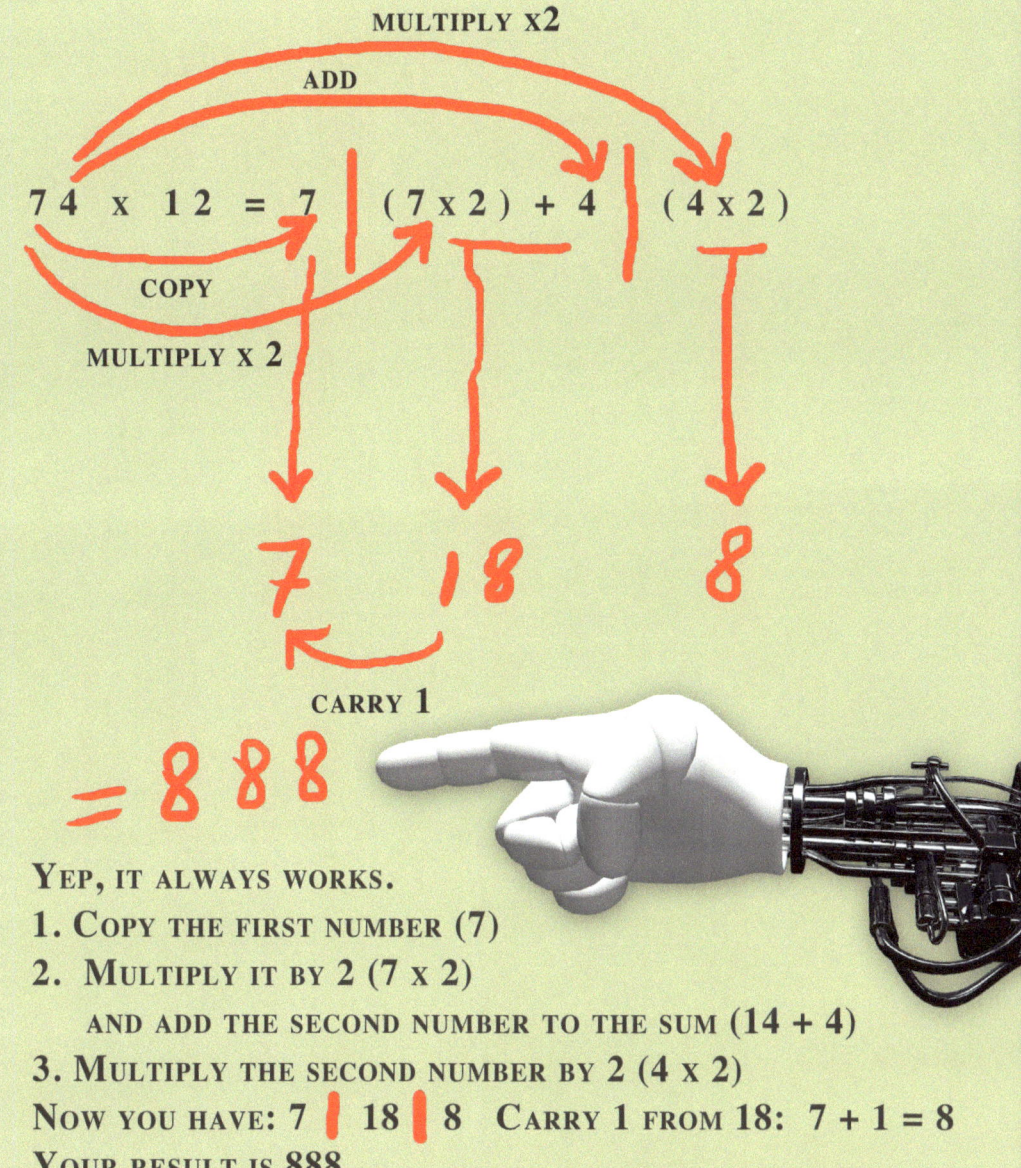

Yep, it always works.
1. Copy the first number (7)
2. Multiply it by 2 (7 x 2)
   and add the second number to the sum (14 + 4)
3. Multiply the second number by 2 (4 x 2)
Now you have: 7 | 18 | 8   Carry 1 from 18: 7 + 1 = 8
Your result is 888
Isn't that cool?

ALSO EASY!

NEXT. TIMES 3.
ADD ANY NUMBER TO ITSELF TWICE.
EASY!
4 x 3 = 4 + 4 + 4 = 12
5 x 3 = 5 + 5 + 5 = 15

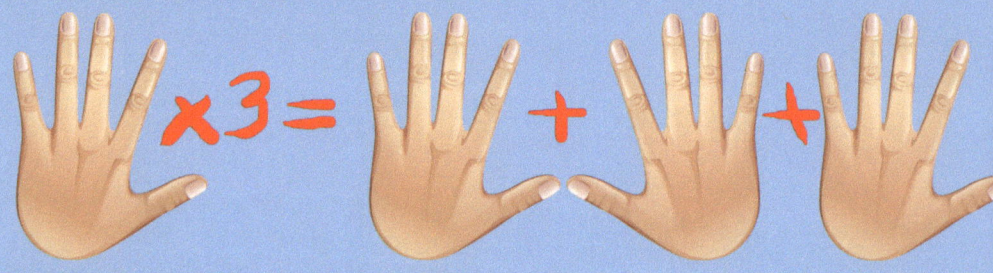

IS THIS EASIER THAN MEMORIZING?
FOR SOME PEOPLE IT IS. AT LEAST IN THE BEGINNING.
BUT YOU MAY WANT TO GO AHEAD AND MEMORIZE THESE:

3 x 3 = 9   8 x 3 = 24
4 x 3 = 12   AND
6 x 3 = 18   12 x 3 = 36
7 x 3 = 21

DO YOU THINK YOU CAN MEMORIZE THEM TODAY?

I SKIPPED 5 - YOU DON'T NEED TO MEMORIZE THAT:
IT'S JUST 3 HANDS / 15 FINGERS.
AND I ALSO SKIPPED 9, 10 AND 11.
YOU ALREADY KNOW OTHER TRICKS FOR THEM.

IF YOUR NUMBERS SWITCH PLACES,
THE RESULT IS STILL THE SAME:
2 x 4 IS THE SAME AS 4 x 2,
3 x 5 IS THE SAME AS 5 x 3.
SO YOU REALLY NEED TO REMEMBER ONLY HALF
OF YOUR TIMES TABLES! TAKE A LOOK AT THE NEXT PAGE!

ONLY HALF!!!

Once you have learned that 2 x 1 = 2, you don't need to learn 1 x 2 - it's the same. Cross it out!

Once you have learned that 3 x 2 = 6, you don't need to learn 2 x 3. Cross it out!

1 x 1 = 1	~~1 x 2 = 2~~	~~1 x 3 = 3~~	~~1 x 4 = 4~~
2 x 1 = 2	2 x 2 = 4	~~2 x 3 = 6~~	~~2 x 4 = 8~~
3 x 1 = 3	3 x 2 = 6	3 x 3 = 9	~~3 x 4 = 12~~
4 x 1 = 4	4 x 2 = 8	4 x 3 = 12	4 x 4 = 16
5 x 1 = 5	5 x 2 = 10	5 x 3 = 15	5 x 4 = 20
6 x 1 = 6	6 x 2 = 12	6 x 3 = 18	6 x 4 = 24
7 x 1 = 7	7 x 2 = 14	7 x 3 = 21	7 x 4 = 28
8 x 1 = 8	8 x 2 = 16	8 x 3 = 24	8 x 4 = 32
9 x 1 = 9	9 x 2 = 18	9 x 3 = 27	9 x 4 = 36
10 x 1 = 10	10 x 2 = 20	10 x 3 = 30	10 x 4 = 40
11 x 1 = 11	11 x 2 = 22	11 x 3 = 33	11 x 4 = 44
12 x 1 = 12	12 x 2 = 24	12 x 3 = 36	12 x 4 = 48

~~1 x 5 = 5~~	~~1 x 6 = 6~~	~~1 x 7 = 7~~	~~1 x 8 = 8~~
~~2 x 5 = 10~~	~~2 x 6 = 12~~	~~2 x 7 = 14~~	~~2 x 8 = 16~~
~~3 x 5 = 15~~	~~3 x 6 = 18~~	~~3 x 7 = 21~~	~~3 x 8 = 24~~
~~4 x 5 = 20~~	~~4 x 6 = 24~~	~~4 x 7 = 28~~	~~4 x 8 = 32~~
5 x 5 = 25	~~5 x 6 = 30~~	~~5 x 7 = 35~~	~~5 x 8 = 40~~
6 x 5 = 30	6 x 6 = 36	~~6 x 7 = 42~~	~~6 x 8 = 48~~
7 x 5 = 35	7 x 6 = 42	7 x 7 = 49	~~7 x 8 = 56~~
8 x 5 = 40	8 x 6 = 48	8 x 7 = 56	8 x 8 = 64
9 x 5 = 45	9 x 6 = 54	9 x 7 = 63	9 x 8 = 72
10 x 5 = 50	10 x 6 = 60	10 x 7 = 70	10 x 8 = 80
11 x 5 = 55	11 x 6 = 66	11 x 7 = 77	11 x 8 = 88
12 x 5 = 60	12 x 6 = 72	12 x 7 = 84	12 x 8 = 96

~~1 x 9 = 9~~	~~1 x 10 = 10~~	~~1 x 11 = 11~~	~~1 x 12 = 12~~
~~2 x 9 = 18~~	~~2 x 10 = 20~~	~~2 x 11 = 22~~	~~2 x 12 = 24~~
~~3 x 9 = 27~~	~~3 x 10 = 30~~	~~3 x 11 = 33~~	~~3 x 12 = 36~~
~~4 x 9 = 36~~	~~4 x 10 = 40~~	~~4 x 11 = 44~~	~~4 x 12 = 48~~
~~5 x 9 = 45~~	~~5 x 10 = 50~~	~~5 x 11 = 55~~	~~5 x 12 = 60~~
~~6 x 9 = 54~~	~~6 x 10 = 60~~	~~6 x 11 = 66~~	~~6 x 12 = 72~~
~~7 x 9 = 63~~	~~7 x 10 = 70~~	~~7 x 11 = 77~~	~~7 x 12 = 84~~
~~8 x 9 = 72~~	~~8 x 10 = 80~~	~~8 x 11 = 88~~	~~8 x 12 = 96~~
9 x 9 = 81	~~9 x 10 = 90~~	~~9 x 11 = 99~~	~~9 x 12 = 108~~
10 x 9 = 90	10 x 10 = 100	~~10 x 11 = 110~~	~~10 x 12 = 120~~
11 x 9 = 99	11 x 10 = 110	11 x 11 = 121	~~11 x 12 = 132~~
12 x 9 = 108	12 x 10 = 120	12 x 11 = 132	12 x 12 = 144

Haha... almost nothing to learn here!

If you Know x3, You know x13!

Times 13 is not in our times tables, but since we are on a roll, I'll teach you x13, and then we'll go back to the baby portion of our times table.

The trick here is the same as in x12, only you multiply your numbers not x2, but x3. So if you have learned your x3 table, you can do x13 easily!

2 x 13 = 2 (2x3) = 26
3 x 13 = 3 (3x3) = 39
4 x 13 = 4 (4x3) = 4 (12) carry 1 = 52
5 x 13 = 5 (5x3) = 5 (15) carry 1 = 65
6 x 13 = 6 (6x3) = 6 (18) carry 1 = 78
7 x 13 = 7 (7x3) = 7 (21) carry 2 = 91
8 x 13 = 8 (8x3) = 8 (24) carry 2 (8+2=10) = 104
9 x 13 = 9 (9x3) = 9 (27) carry 2 (9+2=11) = 117

Totally doable, right? If you have followed me up to here, give yourself a good pat on the back: Not every kid can grasp the tricks of speed math. Excellent job!

Moving On!

Back to easy stuff. <mark>Times 4.</mark>
x 4 is just x 2 + x 2.
So if 3 x 2 = 6
then 3 x 4 = 6 + 6 = 12

If you can do any number x 2, and you can add simple numbers, Times 4 is not worth memorizing. Look:

2 x 2 = 4   2 x 4 = 4 + 4 = 8
3 x 2 = 6   3 x 4 = 6 + 6 = 12
4 x 2 = 8   4 x 4 = 8 + 8 = 16
5 x 2 = 10   5 x 4 = 10 + 10 = 20

Well, maybe you want to memorize just these:

4 x 4 = 16
6 x 4 = 24
7 x 4 = 28
8 x 4 = 32

<mark>Times 5.</mark> Count your fingers:
2 hands = 10 fingers
3 hands = 15 fingers
4 hands = 20 fingers

More than 5 or 6 hands, and you stop to think, so maybe you should memorize these:

5 x 6 = 30
5 x 7 = 35
5 x 8 = 40

When you multiply x 5, your result always ends in 5 or 10.

The Rest of It Right Now!

We've looked at x 0, 1, 2, 3, 4, 5 and x 9, 10, 11, and 12.
What about x 6, 7 and 8?
I've asked many kids and grownups which numbers are the hardest to remember in the times tables.
Most of them agree it's 7 x 8.
Guess what. I can teach you 7 x 8 right now in a way that you will always remember.

Write: 5   6   7   8
Look!   5   6 = 7 × 8
Yes! 7 x 8 = 56   MAGIC!

More good news! Remember how we learned to do x 9 on our fingers? You can do x 6, 7, 8 on your fingers too!
But you need to know x 2, 3, 4 to make this happen.
So, make sure you remember your x 2, 3, 4 tables, and away we go!

Give your fingers numbers. You can even write them on your fingers with a marker or a pen, if you wish.

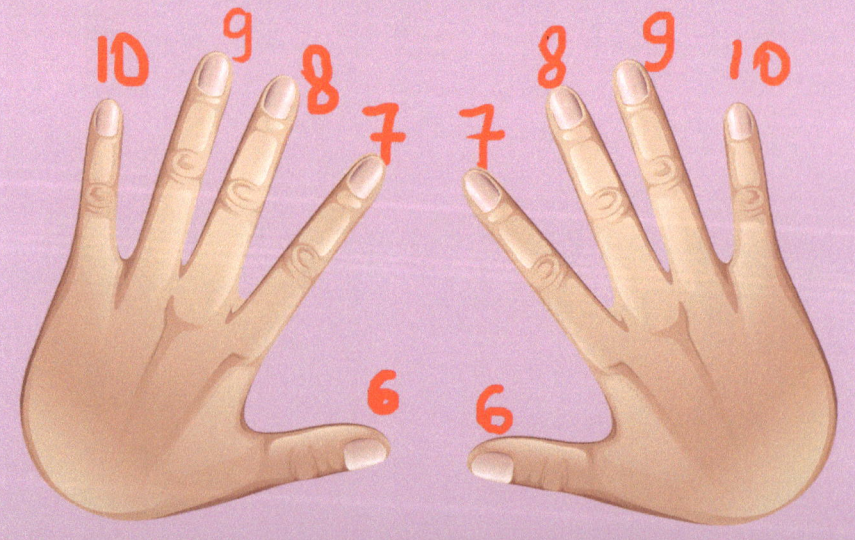

IF YOU WANT TO KNOW **6 x 8**,
JUST CONNECT FINGER **6** WITH FINGER **8**.

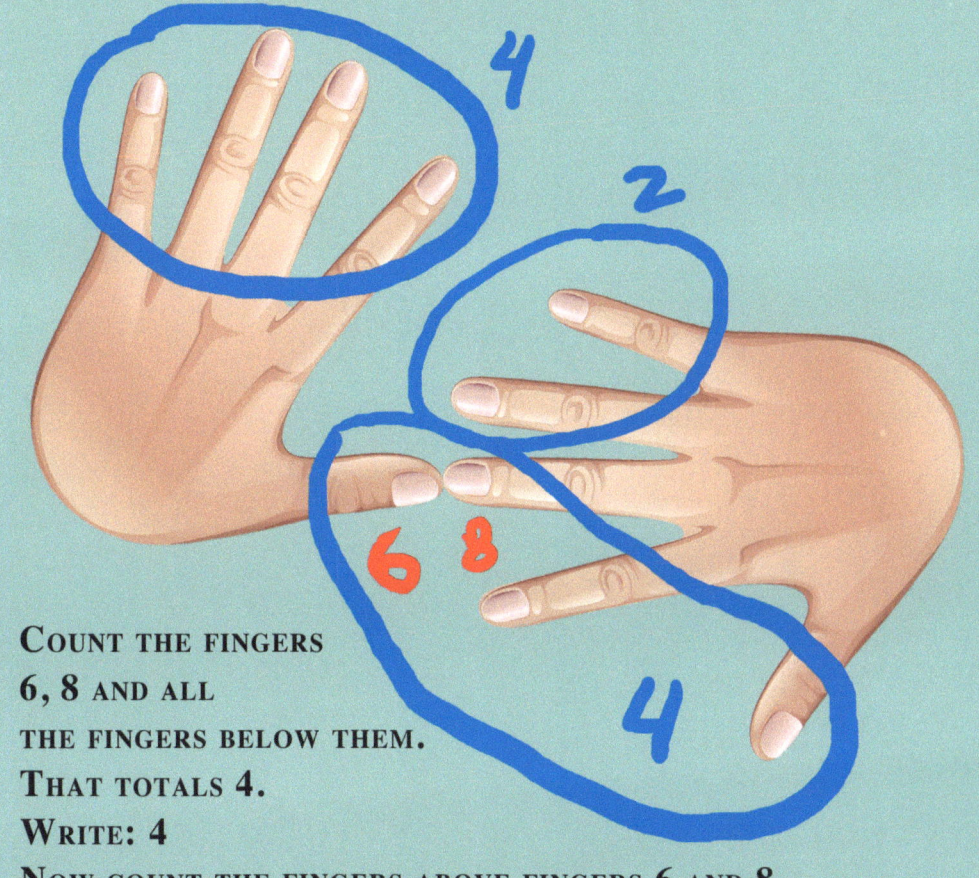

COUNT THE FINGERS
6, 8 AND ALL
THE FINGERS BELOW THEM.
THAT TOTALS **4**.
WRITE: **4**
NOW COUNT THE FINGERS ABOVE FINGERS **6** AND **8**.
THERE ARE **4** ON THE LEFT, AND **2** ON THE RIGHT.
MULTIPLY THEM: **4 x 2 = 8**
SEE, THAT'S WHY YOU NEED THOSE SMALL NUBMER TIMES
TABLES, LIKE X **2, 3, 4, 5**.

YOU RESULT IS: **4 (4x2) = 48**

6 x 8 = 48

IT ALSO RHYMES: SIX TIMES EIGHT - FORTY EIGHT.

LET'S TRY ANOTHER ONE!

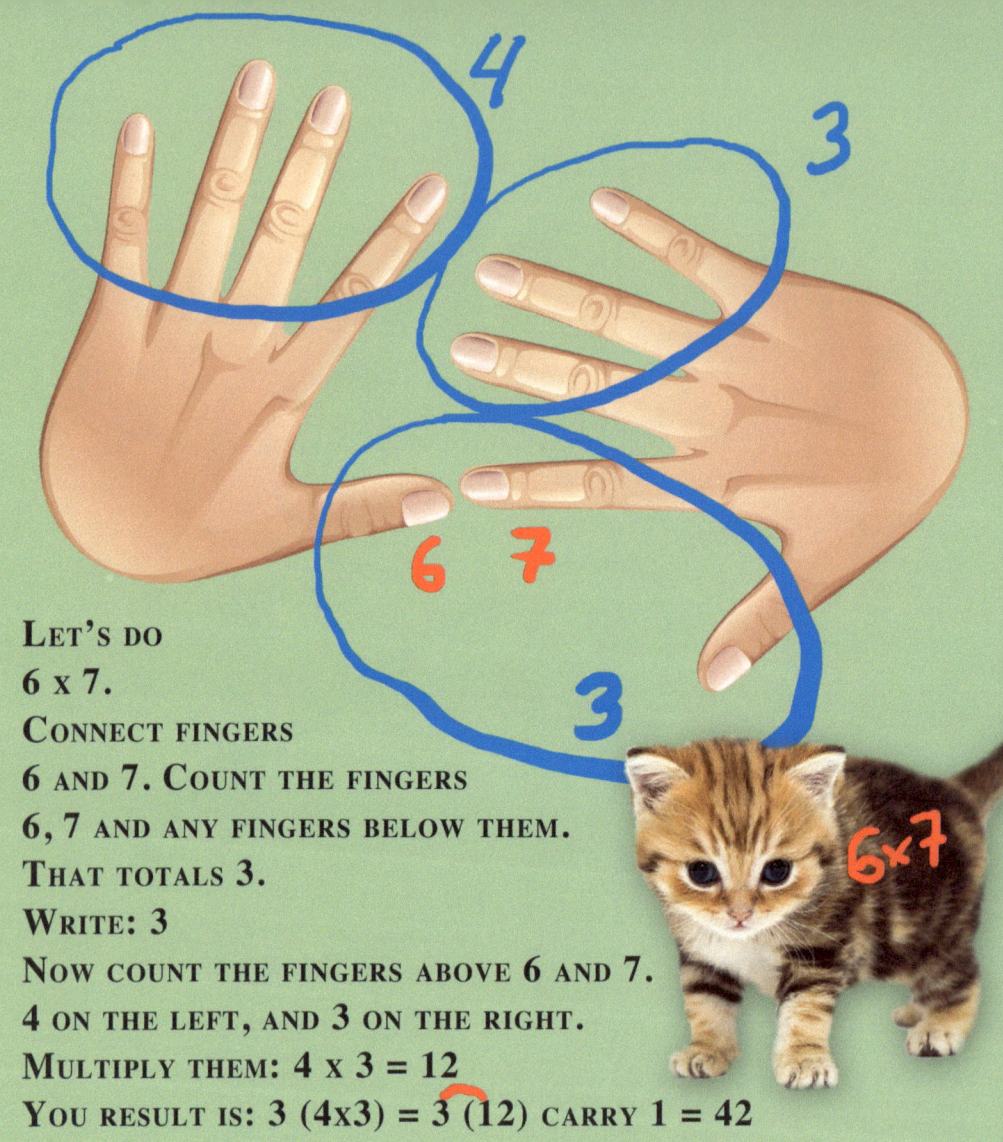

Let's do
6 x 7.
Connect fingers
6 and 7. Count the fingers
6, 7 and any fingers below them.
That totals 3.
Write: 3
Now count the fingers above 6 and 7.
4 on the left, and 3 on the right.
Multiply them: 4 x 3 = 12
You result is: 3 (4x3) = 3 (12) carry 1 = 42

6 x 7 = 42

WE ARE DONE! Done with the times tables!

Reminder: All these tricks are MENTAL CHEAT SHEETS. They help you take control. But sooner or later you need to learn your times tables by heart. Please try to remember as much as you can, and the math monster will purr like a kitten at your feet!

1	2	3	4	5	6	7	8	9	10	11	12
2	4	6	8	10	12	14	16	18	20	22	24
3	6	9	12	15	18	21	24	27	30	33	36
4	8	12	16	20	24	28	32	36	40	44	48
5	10	15	20	25	30	35	40	45	50	55	60
6	12	18	24	30	36	42	48	54	60	66	72
7	14	21	28	35	42	49	56	63	70	77	84
8	16	24	32	40	48	56	64	72	80	88	96
9	18	27	36	45	54	63	72	81	90	99	108
10	20	30	40	50	60	70	80	90	100	110	120
11	22	33	44	55	66	77	88	99	110	121	132
12	24	36	48	60	72	84	96	108	120	132	144

REMEMBER THIS TABLE? HERE IS HOW WE HANDLE IT:

■ BABY STUFF

■ LEARN THIS BY HEART NOW

■ DO THIS ON YOUR FINGERS

■ USE X 11 TRICK

■ USE X 12 TRICK

□ THESE SQUARES ARE JUST A MIRROR REFLECTION OF THE SQUARES I COLORED. JUST IGNORE THEM!

 THE NUMBERS IN THESE RED FRAMES ARE CALLED SQUARES. 4 IS THE SQUARE OF 2, BECAUSE 2 X 2 = 4. A SQUARE IS A NUMBER MULTIPLIED BY ITSELF. TRY TO LEARN THEM FIRST!

CLOCK MAGIC

TIME TO LEARN A NEW MATH MAGIC TRICK!
ASK A PERSON TO CHOOSE ANY HOUR ON THE CLOCK FROM 1 TO 12. THEY SHOULD KEEP THAT NUMBER SECRET. NEXT TELL THEM TO NOTICE WHICH NUMBER IS DIRECTLY OPPOSITE TO THE ONE THEY HAVE CHOSEN.
SO THEY HAVE 2 SECRET NUMBERS NOW.

ASK THEM TO SUBTRACT THE SMALLER NUMBER FROM THE BIGGER NUMBER, THEN MULTIPLY THE RESULT x2 AND ADD 8.
(SECRET#1 – SECRET#2) x 2 + 8 = ?
NOW TELL THEM YOU KNOW THE RESULT.
HOW DO YOU KNOW IT? YOU CAN READ THEIR MIND.
TELL THEM IT'S 20!

SO, MAYBE THEIR SECRET#1 = 10 AND SECRET#2 = 4
(10 – 4) x 2 + 8 = 20
WHAT IF THEIR SECRET#1 = 7 AND SECRET#2 = 1 ?
(7– 1) x 2 + 8 = 20

MAGIC, RIGHT?

HERE'S HOW IT WORKS.

WHEN YOU ASK A PERSON TO COME UP WITH TWO NUMBERS ON THE CLOCK DIRECTLY OPPOSITE EACH OTHER, IT'S THE SAME AS DIVIDING THE CLOCK IN HALF WITH A STRAIGHT LINE, LIKE THIS:

NO MATTER WHAT NUMBERS WERE CHOSEN, THE DIFFERENCE BETWEEN THEM WILL ALWAYS BE HALF THE CLOCK. SINCE ALL CLOCKS SHOW 12 HOURS, THE DIFFERENCE BETWEEN YOUR NUMBERS WILL ALWAYS BE 6.
9 – 3 = 6
10 – 4 = 6

THIS IS VERY SIMPLE, SO, TO MAKE IT MORE MYSTERIOUS, ADD OTHER THINGS, LIKE *MULTIPLY IT X 2 AND ADD 8*.

THIS ADDITIONS CAN BE ANYTHING!

5 AND 10 BREAKDOWN

I like the word *BREAKDOWN*. I like breaking down scary huge numbers into little friendly pieces.

If there is a magic wand in the world of math, it's the breakdown of these two numbers: 5 and 10.

If you break these numbers into pieces, you can use those pieces as magic keys to many amazing tricks. So here we go.

5 = 1 + 4   or
5 = 2 + 3   These are the pieces that make up 5!

10 = 1 + 9
10 = 2 + 8
10 = 3 + 7
10 = 4 + 6
10 = 5 + 5

These are the pieces that make up 10.

They also call these magic pieces *COMPLEMENTS*. They complement (add to) each other to make a 10. For example, 4 is the complement of 6. Don't confuse them with *COMPLIMENTS*! A *COMPLIMENT* is a nice thing you say, like *Wow, you are really good at math!*

Can you check if you remember these sets? Cover the numbers above with your hand, and finish these sentences:

10 = 1 + ...
10 = 2 + ...
10 = 3 + ...
10 = 4 + ...
10 = 5 + ...

Done? Now let's see how we can use these magic pieces to speed up our addition.

MAKE A 10!

SO OFTEN YOU SEE A MATH PROBLEM THAT LOOKS HARD AND HORRIBLE, AND THEN YOU NOTICE THESE MAGIC PIECES OF 10 SPARKLING RIGHT IN THE MIDDLE OF IT LIKE RARE GEMS! IF YOU SPOT THEM, GRAB THEM AND MAKE A 10!

FOR EXAMPLE, YOU ARE STARING AT THIS, HOPELESSLY:
$3 + 12 + 9 + 7 + 1 = ?$
SUDDENLY YOU NOTICE: 3 AND 7, 9 AND 1.
IN NO TIME, YOU KNOW THAT IT'S
$10 + 10 + 12 = 32$ IT'S A PIECE OF CAKE.

THESE PIECES OF 10 ARE NEVER IN ORDER IN MATH PROBLEMS. THEY ARE ALWAYS SCATTERED ALL OVER. WHY?
DON'T ASK ME!
I DON'T KNOW WHO COMES UP WITH PROBLEMS FOR KIDS' MATH TESTS!

> I WILL SCATTER ALL THESE PIECES, SO KIDS CAN'T SOLVE THIS! MUA-HA-HA-HA!

SAME WITH SUBTRACTION.
TAKE A LOOK AT
THIS BEAUTY:
$59 - 4 - 17 - 8 - 16 - 2 = ?$

IF I DIDN'T KNOW ABOUT THE MAGIC PIECES OF 10, I WOULD HAVE CRIED. BUT SINCE I KNOW ABOUT THEM, FIRST THING I DO IS LOOK FOR THESE GEMS. AND I FIND THEM:
16 AND 4, 8 AND 2 - TOGETHER THESE PIECES MAKE 30.
SO NOW I CAN DO IT IN MY HEAD, REAL FAST $59 - 30 - 17 = 12$.

8 AND 9

My favorite numbers to add or subtract are 9 and 8. You know why? They are really close to 10.
10 = 9 + 1 and 10 = 8 + 2

So if I have any number ending in 9 in my math problem, I just replace it with 10, and then simply add 1 or take away 1 from my result. Like this:
37 − 19 = ?
Replace 9 with 10: 37 − 20 = 17
Add 1: 17 + 1 = 18   Sooooo easy!

Same with 8. 75 + 18 = ?
Replace 8 with 10: 75 + 20 = 95
Take away 2:   95 − 2 = 93

Freedom! Homework done!

CLOSE TO 100

THIS TRICK WORKS GREAT WHEN YOUR NUMBERS GET REAL CLOSE TO 100. FOR EXAMPLE:
98 + 75 = YUCK!
HOLD ON! JUST THINK: 98 IS ONLY 2 LESS THAN 100, SO REPLACE IT WITH 100:
100 + 75 = 175
AND THEN TAKE AWAY 2:
175 − 2 = 173
THAT'S WHAT I CALL EASY!

AND AS LONG AS YOU REMEMBER WHICH MAGIC PIECES MAKE UP 10, YOU CAN DO THIS TRICK WITH ANY NUMBERS, NOT JUST NUMBERS ENDING IN 9 OR 8.
HOW ABOUT THIS PROBEM:

NINA HAS CAUGHT 94 CENTIPEDES TO SCARE HER GRANDMA. MARK HAS CAPTURED 59 LADY BUGS TO SCARE HIS GRANDPA. THEY PUT CENTIPEDES AND LADY BUGS TOGETHER IN THE SAME JAR TO SEE WHO WINS, CENTIPEDES OR LADY BUGS.
HOW MANY BUGS ARE IN THE JAR?

94 + 59 = EW! RUN! TOO MANY BUGS!!!

NOW THINK: 94 IS 6 LESS THAN 100.
REPLACE IT WITH 100: 100 + 59 = 159
NOW TAKE AWAY 6: 159 − 6 = 153

HAVE YOU EVER NOTICED THEY ALWAYS ASK THE WRONG QUESTIONS IN MATH PROBLEMS? WHO CARES HOW MANY BUGS ARE IN THE JAR? WHAT WE WANT TO KNOW IS:
DID THE CENTIPEDES EAT THE LADY BUGS?

SAME THING WITH SUBTRACTION.
I AWAYS KEEP MY EYES OPEN FOR
ANY NUMBERS ANYWHERE CLOSE TO 100.

647 - 298 LOOKS TOTALLY IMPOSSIBLE.

> OH NO!
> IT'S 3-DIGITS!

> I'LL HAVE TO
> DO IT ON PAPER...
> I'LL HAVE TO CARRY,
> I'LL HAVE TO BORROW...
> HELP!....

YOU FEEL HOPELESS, UNTIL YOU NOTICE THAT
298 IS ONLY 2 LESS THAN 300!
REPLACE IT WITH 300, QUICK!
647 – 300 = 347 AND NOW GIVE BACK 2
THE ANSWER IS 349! JUST LIKE THAT.
SEE? AND YOU WERE ABOUT TO GIVE UP!

THE BORDER TRICK

IF YOU HAVE A SUBTRACTION PROBLEM WITH 2 BIG NUMBERS, IT HELPS TO SEE IF THERE IS ANY CLEAR-CUT BORDER SOMEWEHRE BETWEEN THESE NUMBERS.

FOR EXAMPLE, IF WE HAVE:
137 – 85 = ?
WE CAN THINK OF 100 AS THE BORDER: OUR NUMBERS ARE ON DIFFERENT SIDES OF THIS BORDER, AND WE NEED TO FIND THE DISTANCE BETWEEN THEM.

37 + 15 = 52

WHEN WE SUBTRACT, WE FIND THE DIFFERENCE BETWEEN 2 NUMBERS. YOU CAN THINK OF THAT DIFFERENCE AS THE DISTANCE OF BOTH NUMBERS FROM THE BORDER.
IF DISTANCES FROM THE BORDER ARE 37 AND 15,
WE CAN SAY: 37 + 15 = 52
THAT'S THE SAME AS 137 – 85 = 52

SO IN MANY PROBLEMS <u>YOU CAN JUST REPLACE SUBTRACTION WITH ADDITION.</u> LET'S DO 67 – 39. OUR BORDER WILL BE 50.

67 — 17
---------- 50   17 + 11 = 28
39 — 11   67 – 39 = 28

Break Them! Don't Carry!

Get used to breaking numbers into pieces. Numbers only look scary when they are big. Small numbers are easy!

One way to add numbers fast is to add tens and ones separately.

2-digit numbers are hard!

If you see something like this:

95 + 13 + 47   *SCARY!*

Add the tens first: 90 + 10 + 40 = 140
Then the ones: 5 + 3 + 7 = 15
Now add ones to tens: 140 + 15 = 145.

You can do this all in your head! It's much faster than doing it on paper:

```
  95
  13
+ 47
-----
```
SCARY!

Try it! You have to carry 1 from ones to tens, then you have to carry 1 from tens to hundreds... Eyaah!

Try this one in your head: 54 + 25 + 16 = ?

Tens: 80 **Ones:** 15 **Answer:** 95!

3-digit numbers? No way...

How about 386 + 429 = ?

Are you scared? Relax!
300 + 400 = 700
80 + 20 = 100
6 + 9 = 15
700 + 100 + 15 = 815

THE BIG FAT ZERO

Let's go back to multiplication, and test a few more secret speed math tricks.

First, let's get zero out of the way once and for all. Zero is a **BIG FAT NOTHING!**
Remember how we did x 10? We just write a **0** at the end of any number we multiply by 10, like 5 x 10 = 50.

The same method works with all zeros everywhere. To do 250 x 20, first drop the 2 zeros, do 25 x 2 = 50, and then bring back the zeros: 5,000.
See?
One more example: 7,000 x 110
Drop the 4 zeros, do 7 x 11 = 77
Now bring back all 4 zeros: 770,000.

As I said: These zeros are a **BIG FAT ZERO**.

Easy! Nothing to do here. I love it!

NINETY THIS X NINETY THAT

IF YOU ARE MULTIPLYING TWO NUMBERS, BOTH JUST BELOW 100, YOU DON'T EVEN NEED TO THINK!
A LADY BUG CAN DO THIS!

LET'S DO: 98 x 97 = ?

98 IS 2 AWAY FROM 100
97 IS 3 AWAY FROM 100

MAKE A BUTTERFLY LIKE THIS:

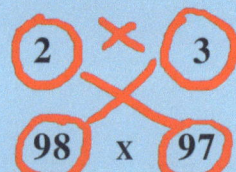

NOW SUBTRACT 98 – 3 OR 97 – 2.
THE RESULT WILL BE THE SAME, 95. WRITE IT DOWN.

95

NEXT, MULTIPLY THE TOP NUMBERS IN THE BUTTERFLY
2 x 3 = 6 WRITE 6 NEXT TO 95.

956

THIS IS OUR RESULT! 98 x 97 = 956
YOU CAN DO IT IN YOUR HEAD! IN YOUR SLEEP!

LET'S TRY ANOTHER ONE 92 x 96.

92 x 96   92 – 4 = 88 | 8 x 4 = 32 | 92 x 96 = **8832**

Just Above 100

Next, let's multily numbers above 100, but still close to 100.
100 is our base.
112 x 109

112 x 109 Hmmmm... Catching mice is easier!

112 is 12 above 100.
109 is 9 above 100.
Here is our butterfly again.

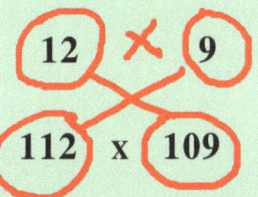

Add 2 numbers crisscross inside the butterfly:
112 + 9 or 109 + 12 = 121
Now multiply the top numbers in the butterfly:
12 x 9 = 108

Add the results, shifting the first number 2 digits to the left, since our base is 100.

12100
+ 108
12208   112 x 109 = 12208

One more example: 115 x 102

Butterfly? It doesn't look anything like me!

115 + 2 = 117   15 x 2 = 30   11700 + 30 = 11730

It's Magic!

Tell your friend to think of a number from 1 to 9.
They should keep it secret.
Then tell them to double it – in their head, secretly!
Next, they should add 2.
Next multiply the result by 5.
And take away 7.

Next tell them you know the answer!
Say: "It's a 2-digit number where
- the first digit is the first number you came up with
- and the second digit is 3!"

Try it:
My number is 7.
Next you tell me to double it: 7 x 2 = 14
Add 2 :   14 + 2 = 16
Multiply by 5:   16 x 5 = 80
Take away 7:   80 - 7 = 73   !!!!!!   I told ya!

Teen Multiplication

Sometimes you need to quickly multiply 2-digit numbers that are in the teens. For example: 13 x 14 or 17 x 15. Here is how you do this, using these numbers' distance from 10.

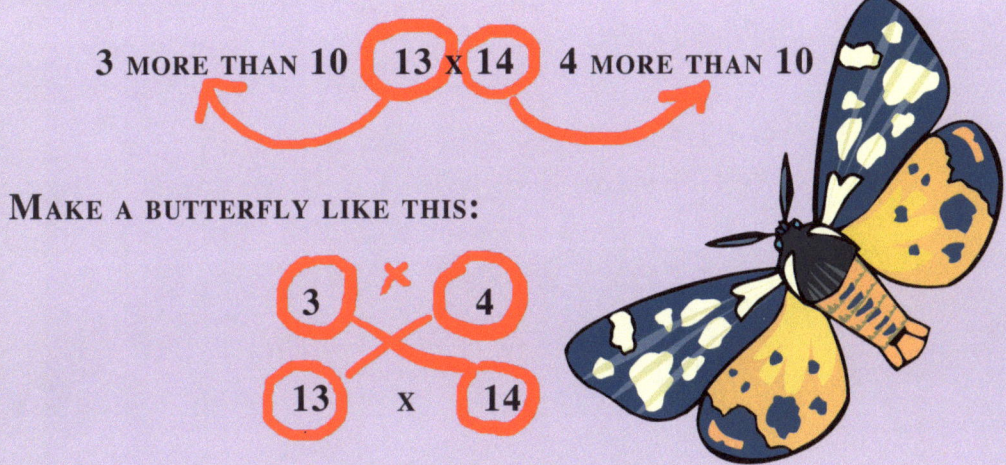

Make a butterfly like this:

We'll use this hundreds / tens / ones box:

HUNDREDS	TENS	ONES

Tens:
Add 2 numbers in the butterfly crisscross:
13 + 4 or 14 + 3 (same result) = 17

Ones:
Multiply the top row of the butterfly: 3 x 4 = 12

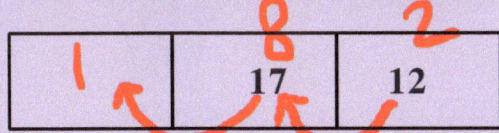

Carry 1 from the ones to the tens, and 1 from the tens to the hundreds. The answer is 182.

BREAK YOUR TEEN NUMBERS!

WHAT IF ONE OF YOUR NUMBERS IS IN THE TEENS, AND ONE IS SMALLER THAN 10?
LIKE 17 x 9 ?
THE EASIEST WAY TO DO THIS IS TO BREAK YOUR TEEN NUMBER INTO 10 + 7 AND <u>MULTIPLY EACH PIECE</u> x 9
(10 x 9) + (7 x 9) = 90 + 63 = 153

NOW TRY 56 x 7
(50 x 7) + (6 x 7) = ...

50 x 7 - DROP THE ZERO, DO 5 x 7 = 35, THEN ADD BACK THE ZERO = 350.
NOW DO 6 x 7 = 42
350 + 42 = 392

> THIS IS SUPPOSED TO BE EASY??

EVEN IF YOU HAVE SOME MONSTROUS 3-DIGIT NUMBER, YOU CAN EASILY MULTIPLY IT PIECE BY PIECE:
457 x 9 = (400 x 9) + (50 x 9) + (7 x 9)
400 x 9 DROP THE ZEROS: 4 x 9 = 36
ADD BACK THE ZEROS 3600
50 x 9 DROP THE ZERO 5 x 9 = 45,
ADD BACK THE ZERO = 450
7 x 9 = 63
3600
 450
+ 63

4113

> OOPS... I TAKE IT BACK... THAT WASN'T EASY AT ALL!

STOP! DON'T RUN AWAY!
<u>I'LL SHOW YOU A MAGIC TRICK!</u>

THE SPOOKY 1089

ASK A FRIEND TO ✓ COME UP WITH ANY 3-DIGIT NUMBER WHERE THE DIGITS GO FROM BIG TO SMALL, LIKE 973. TELL THEM TO KEEP IT SECRET. THIS IS THEIR NUMBER 1. NOW THEY SHOULD SECRETLY DO THIS:

✓ WRITE NUMBER 1 IN REVERSE. THIS WILL BE THEIR NUMBER 2.
✓ SUBTRACT THE REVERSED NUMBER FROM THEIR ORIGINAL NUMBER. THIS IS THEIR NUMBER 3.
✓ WRITE NUMBER 3 IN REVERSE. THIS WILL BE THEIR NUMBER 4.
✓ ADD NUMBERS 3 AND 4.

TELL THEM YOU KNOW THE RESULT. IT'S **1089**.

GUESS WHAT. NO MATTER WHAT NUMBER THEY SELECT IN THE BEGINNING, THE RESULT WILL ALWAYS BE 1089. CRAZY!

NUMBER 1 = 973
NUMBER 2: 379
973 - 379 = 594
IN REVERSE: 495
594 + 495 = 1089

LET'S TEST IT:
721 - 127 = 594   594 + 495 = 1089   SPOOKY!
965 - 569 = 396   396 + 693 = 1089   CREEPY!
WEIRD! EERIE! GHOSTLY! SPINE-CHILLING!

9 Is The Secret

How does that **1089** trick work?
Don't ask me! Well, actually, I asked my Dad who is a mathematician. And he wrote this for me...
If math still scares you, close your eyes!
And skip a few lines down!

Any 3-digit number $100a + 10b + c$,
where $10 > a > b > c$
Reversed number: $100c + 10b + a$
Subtract them: $100a + c - 100c - a = 99(a - c)$,
Let's write $a - c$ *as* y, $a - c = y$
Number $99y$ *can be presented as:*
$100y - y = 100y - 100 + 100 - y = 100(y - 1) + 90 + 10 - y$
The reversed number is: $(10 - y)100 + 90 + y - 1$
Their sum is:
$100y - 100 + 90 + 10 - y + 1000 - 100y + 90 + y - 1 =$
$= 1000 + 90 - 1 = 1089$

Whew! Wow, that was scary!
From what I understand, the simple explanation is this:
The trick is based on the x **9**.
$1089 = 9 \times 121$
That's why there is a simpler version of this trick.
Instead of a 3-digit number, ask your friend to come up with a **2-digit number**, and their end result will be not **1089**, but **99**. The secret is the same:
$9 \times 11 = 99$
So they come up with a 2-digit number, say, 37
Reverse it: 73. Subtract the smaller number from the bigger number: $73 - 37 = 36$. Reverse again: 63
Add them: $36 + 63 = 99$!

Spooky!!!

Square Ending in 5

Remember, a square is any number multiplied by itself, like 3 x 3 = 9, or 7 x 7 = 49

I know a trick that helps you to instantly figure out the square of any number ending in 5, like 55 x 55 or 75 x 75

The result will always end in 25! Think of your result as having 2 parts - left and right. In the right box just write 25.

L [   ] [25] R

To figure out what's on the left, multiply your tens digit by the number one digit higher. So if we do 75 x 75, take 7 and multiply it by 8.

7 x 8 = 56 Place that number on the left.

[56] [25]

75 x 75 = 5625

How about 25 x 25? Your tens digit is 2, the next number is 3, so we go 2 x 3 = 6 Write 25 at the end. Your answer is 625!

So easy! Life is good...

ANY 2-DIGIT SQUARE ANYWHERE!

THERE IS ALSO A TRICK TO QUICKLY FIGURE OUT THE SQUARE OF ANY 2-DIGIT NUMBER. LET'S DO 32 x 32.

THE ANSWER WILL HAVE HUNDREDS, TENS, AND ONES.

HUNDREDS	TENS	ONES

HUNDREDS PLACE:
SQUARE THE FIRST DIGIT.
3 x 3 = 9

TENS PLACE:
MULTIPLY THE FIRST DIGIT BY THE SECOND DIGIT, AND MULTIPLY YOUR RESULT x 2.
3 x 2 = 6
6 x 2 = 12

ONES PLACE:
SQUARE THE LAST DIGIT.
2 x 2 = 4

HUNDREDS	TENS	ONES
9	12	4

I CAN DO IT!

CARRY 1 FROM THE TENS TO THE HUNDREDS PLACE.
THE ANSWER IS 1024.

78 x 78 = ?

7 x 7 = 49	7 x 8 x 2 = 112	8 x 8 = 64	78 x 78 = 6084
49	112	64	
CARRY 11		CARRY 6	

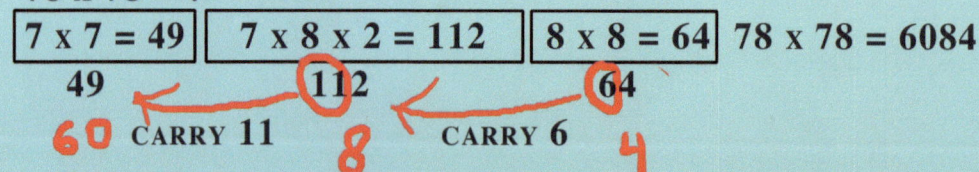

Umbrella

I know it's scary to even think about this, but what if you need to multiply any two 2-digit numbers? I have a trick for this! It's called an Umbrella. Let's do 42 x 37.

1. Multiply the left digits of each number 4 x 3 = 12
2. Multiply the right digits of each number 2 x 7 = 14
3. Write them in this box:

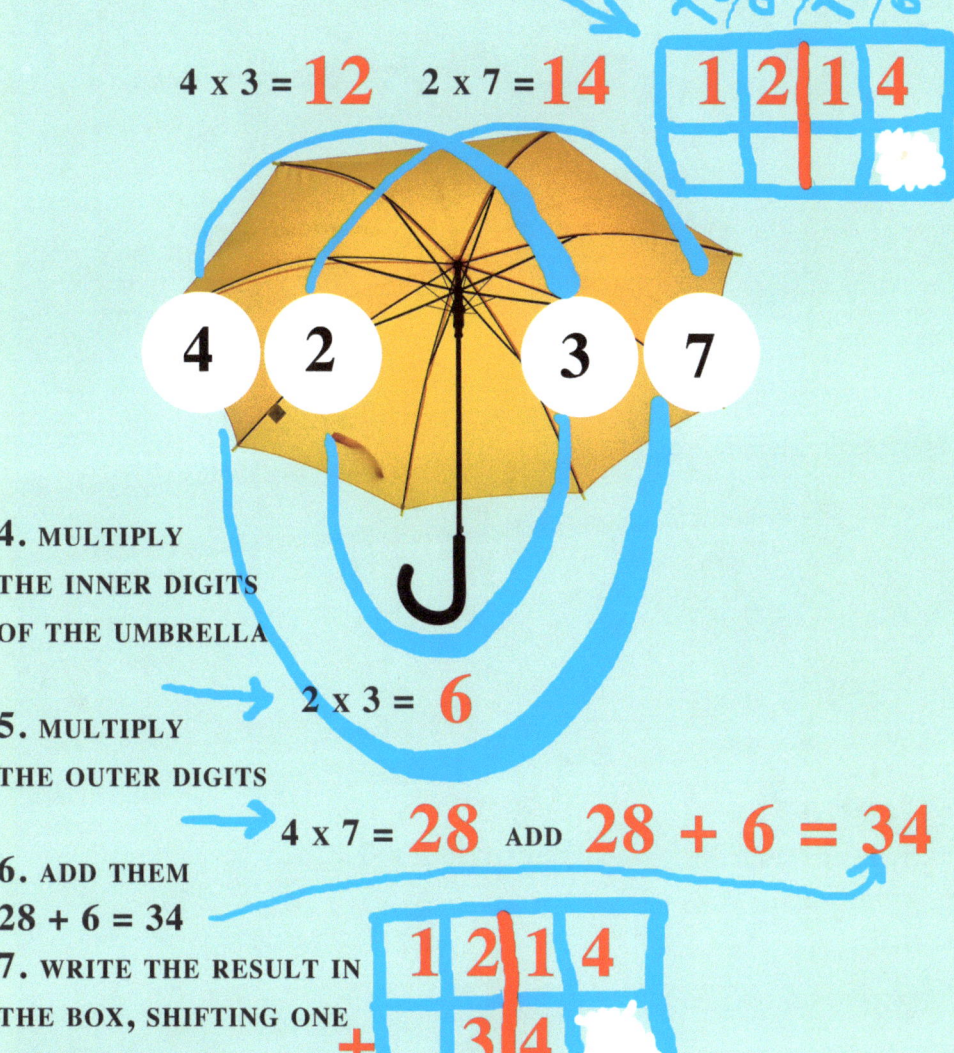

4. Multiply the inner digits of the umbrella

    2 x 3 = 6

5. Multiply the outer digits

    4 x 7 = 28   add   28 + 6 = 34

6. Add them 28 + 6 = 34
7. Write the result in the box, shifting one space left and add these numbers! That's it!

SOMETIMES YOUR NUMBERS ARE SMALLER, AND YOU HAVE SOME EMPTY SPACES IN YOUR BOX. FOR EXAMPLE: 23 x 12

1. MULTIPLY THE LEFT DIGITS 2 x 1 = 2
2. MULTIPLY THE RIGHT DIGITS 3 x 2 = 6
3. WRITE THEM IN THE BOX

2 x 1 = 2   3 x 2 = 6

3 x 1 = 3

2 x 2 = 4   ADD 3 + 4 = 7

4. MULTIPLY THE INNER DIGITS 3 x 1 = 3
5. MULTIPLY THE OUTER DIGITS 2 x 2 = 4.
6. ADD THE INNER AND OUTER RESULTS: 3 + 4 = 7
7. WRITE THE RESULT IN THE BOX SHIFTING ONE SPACE LEFT AND ADD!

2 7 6

DIVISION

If you divide 6 cupcakes among 3 kids, each kid gets 2 cupcakes, and there are no more cupcakes left.

If you divide 6 cupcakes among 4 kids, each kid gets 1 cupcake, and you have 2 more cupcakes left. Those 2 cupcakes are called the *remainder*. We write it like this: R2
6 ÷ 4 = 1 R2

MULTIPLICATION IN REVERSE

DIVISION IS NOT HARD.
IT'S JUST MULTIPLICATION IN REVERSE.
IF YOU KNOW YOUR TIMES TABLES, RELAX: IT WILL BE EASY!
THE ONLY THING DIFFERENT ABOUT DIVISION IS REMAINDERS.

SO IF I AM DIVIDING 32 CUPCAKES AMONG 8 KIDS, I THINK:
HOW MANY 8S WILL FIT INTO 32? AND I START GOING OVER MY
x8 TABLE IN MY HEAD, UNTIL I AM AROUND 32.
32 DIVIDES EVENLY INTO 4:

$32 \div 8 = 4$
$8 \times 4 = 32$

EACH OF THE 8 KIDS GETS 4 CUPCAKES!

BUT IF I AM DIVIDING 33 CUPCAKES,
I WILL NOTICE THAT
33 IS 32 + 1, SO
$33 \div 8 = 4 \text{ r}1$ OR
$33 \div 8 = 8 \times 4 + 1$
... MEANING THAT
ONE CUPCAKE IS LEFT OVER.

I WANT IT!

The Ghost of 5

Time to learn a new magic trick (or two)!

Tell a friend to pick a number from 1 to 10, and keep it secret!
Next tell them to:
1. multiply it by 2
2. add 10 to the result
3. divide this new number by 2
4. take away the very first number they came up with.

Then tell them you know their final number is 5! Hahaha! No matter what number they choose, at the start, the final number will always be 5!
Let's try it with 7:

7 x 2 = 14
14 + 10 = 24
24 ÷ 2 = 12
12 − 7 = 5

The Mysterious 6.

Tell a friend to think of any number, and keep it secret. It's best if they choose a 1-digit number, because they will have to multiply and divide it.
Then tell them:
- ✔ Double your number.
- ✔ Add 12 to the result.
- ✔ Divide it by 2.
- ✔ Take away the first number you came up with.

When they have their answer,
give them that look, like,
I can read your thoughts!
and say:
You are thinking of the number 6, aren't you?
Watch their surprise!
Hahahahaha!
No matter what number they picked at the beginning, they will always end up with a 6 at the end!

Let's try it with 5:

$5 \times 2 = 10$

$10 + 12 = 22$

$22 \div 2 = 11$

$11 - 5 = 6$

FRACTIONS

Oh boy, here they come – Fractions. Try not to panic: we've got some tricks to help you defeat them!

> I am a fraction! I'll get you!

> Oh no. Not this.

NOT REALLY SCARY!

DON'T BE SCARED OF FRACTIONS. THE WHOLE POINT OF BEING A FRACTION IS BEING SMALL! FRACTIONS DON'T ATTACK HUMANS: THEY ARE AFRAID OF YOU!

WHICH IS SCARIER:
A WHOLE APPLE OR HALF AN APPLE?
WELL, HALF AN APPLE IS A FRACTION! IT'S 1/2 OF AN APPLE!
AND IF YOU CUT A WHOLE APPLE INTO 4 PIECES,
EACH OF THOSE PIECES IS 1/4 OF AN APPLE!

WHAT SCARES A LOT OF PEOPLE ABOUT FRACTIONS,
ARE THE LONG WORDS WE USE TO REFER TO THE 2 NUMBERS IN A FRACTION.
THE FIRST (OR THE TOP ONE) IS CALLED THE *NUMERATOR*.
THE SECOND (OR THE BOTTOM ONE) IS CALLED THE *DENOMINATOR*.
IN 1/2, 1 IS A NUMERATOR, AND 2 IS A DENOMINATOR.
YOU CAN WRITE IT LIKE THIS;

1/2   OR LIKE THIS   1/2   OR LIKE THIS $\frac{1}{2}$

1/2 SIMPLY MEANS THAT YOU ARE DIVIDING 1 BY 2
1/4 MEANS THAT YOU ARE DIVIDING 1 BY 4, AND SO ON.

FRACTIONS ARE DIVISION.
20/10 IS 20 DIVIDED BY 10
20 ÷ 10 = 2

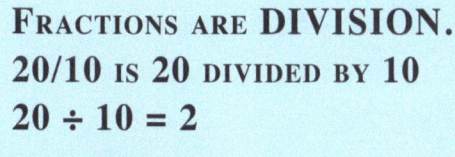

I AM STILL SCARED.

Adding or Subtracting Fractions

Sometimes you don't have 3 cupcakes. You have only 1.
So you cut it in half, and then into 4 pieces.

Now you can think of the cupcake as 4/4
The first 4 is how many pieces you actually have,
The second 4 is into how many pieces you cut it
in the beginning.

So, to begin with, you have all 4 pieces,
but next you need to divide the cupcake among 3 kids.
Each kid gets one piece, 1/4 of a cupcake.
So, together, the kids eat 3 of the 4 pieces you got.
They eat 3/4 of the cupcake.
And one more piece remains for mom —
one of the 4 pieces we had, 1/4.
So if they asked me, How many pieces are left?
I had 4/4 - the whole cupcake cut into 4 pieces.
Kids ate 3/4.
4/4 − 3/4 = 1/4 Mom gets one piece too.
If the bottom number (denominator) in both fractions
is the same, you just add or subtract the top numbers.

$$\frac{4}{4} - \frac{3}{4} = \frac{1}{4}$$

Fraction Adding Trick

What if you have fractions with a different bottom numbers (denominators)?
Like:

$$\frac{3}{5} + \frac{1}{3} = ?$$

Here is an amazing trick to solve this!
To find the **top number, multiply criss-cross:**
5 × 1 = 5 and 3 × 3 = 9, and **add them together** 5 + 9 = 14
Write 14 at the top

$$\frac{3}{5} + \frac{1}{3} = \frac{14}{15}$$

To find the new bottom number, just **multiply the old bottom numbers:** 5 × 3 = 15

Whew! Easy!
Try 2/9 + 3/4

$$\frac{2}{9} + \frac{3}{4} = \frac{35}{36}$$

Top number:
(2 × 4) + (9 × 3) = 8 + 27 = 35
Bottom number: 9 × 4 = 36

Not so scary anymore!

EVEN EASIER!

CHECK THIS OUT!
IF YOU ARE ADDING 2 FRACTIONS, AND BOTH OF THEM HAVE 1 AS THE TOP NUMBER, THEN

ADD THE BOTTOM NUMBERS TO FIND YOUR NEW TOP NUMBER...

AND **MULTIPLY** THE BOTTOM NUMBERS TO FIND YOUR NEW BOTTOM NUMBER!

$$\frac{1}{5} + \frac{1}{3} = \frac{5+3}{5 \times 3} = \frac{8}{15}$$

$$\frac{1}{4} + \frac{1}{7} = \frac{4+7}{4 \times 7} = \frac{11}{28}$$

IF THIS IS NOT EASY, WHAT IS?

So true!

SUBTRACT THEM!

FRACTION SUBTRACTION - IT RHYMES! AND IT'S EASY! HERE IS HOW TO DO IT.

$$\frac{3}{4} - \frac{2}{7} = \frac{(3 \times 7) - (2 \times 4)}{4 \times 7} = \frac{21 - 8}{28}$$

$$= \boxed{\frac{13}{28}}$$

TOP NUMBER:
MULTIPLY CRISS-CROSS:
1ST TOP NUMBER x 2ND BOTTOM NUMBER 3 x 7 = 21
1ST BOTTOM NUMBER x 2ND TOP NUMBER 4 x 2 = 8
SUBTRACT THE SECOND RESULT FROM THE FIRST.

BOTTOM NUMBER:
JUST MULTIPLY THE 1ST BOTTOM NUMBER
BY THE 2ND BOTTOM NUMBER 4 x 7 = 28

AND IF BOTH FRACTIONS HAVE 1 ON TOP, LIKE

$$\frac{1}{2} - \frac{1}{7} = \frac{7 - 2}{2 \times 7} = \frac{5}{14}$$

TO FIND THE **TOP NUMBER:**
SUBTRACT THE 1ST BOTTOM NUMBER
FROM THE 2ND BOTTOM NUMBER 7 - 2 = 5
TO FIND THE **BOTTOM NUMBER:**
MULTIPLY THE BOTTOM NUMBERS: 2 x 7 = 14

MULTIPLY THEM!

$\frac{3}{7} \times \frac{2}{5}$

"My enemies are multiplying!"

"Not a big deal."

I don't assume you are looking forward to multiplying fractions. But maybe you should! Becaue it's so easy it looks like a trick!

When multiplying fractions, to find the **TOP NUMBER**, multiply the top numbers. To find the **BOTTOM NUMBER**, multiply the bottom numbers. That's it!

$$\frac{3}{7} \times \frac{2}{5} = \frac{3 \times 2}{7 \times 5} = \frac{6}{35}$$

DIVIDE THEM!

DIVIDING FRACTIONS? HAHAHAHA! YOU SIMPLY WON'T BELIEVE HOW EASY THIS IS. IT'S THE SAME AS MULTIPLYING FRACTIONS, EXCEPT YOU NEED TO MULTIPLY TOP AND BOTTOM NUMBERS CRISS-CROSS!

$$\frac{2}{7} \div \frac{1}{3} = \frac{2 \times 3}{7 \times 1} = \frac{6}{7}$$

IT'S THAT EASY!

Meow! Let's be friends!

THINGS TO REMEMBER WHEN WORKING WITH FRACTIONS:

1. IF THE TOP NUMBER OF YOUR RESULT IS BIGGER THAN THE BOTTOM NUMBER, DIVIDE THE TOP BY THE BOTTOM:

$$\frac{15}{5} = 3 \qquad \frac{12}{5} = 2\frac{2}{5}$$

15 ÷ 5   12 ÷ 5 = 2 R2

2. IF THE BOTTOM NUMBER CAN BE DIVIDED BY THE TOP NUMBER, DIVIDE BOTH BY THE TOP NUMBER!

$$\frac{3}{15} = \frac{1}{5} \qquad \frac{2}{4} = \frac{1}{2}$$

3 ÷ 3 = 1   15 ÷ 3 = 5   2 ÷ 2 = 1   4 ÷ 2 = 2

3. IF BOTH THE TOP AND BOTTOM NUMBERS CAN BE DIVIDED BY SOME OTHER NUMBER, DO IT!

CAN BE DIVIDED BY ③

$$\frac{15}{27} = \frac{5}{9}$$

15 ÷ 3   27 ÷ 3

I NEVER KNEW I WAS THIS SMART

You can turn any fraction into a decimal.
Just divide the top number by the bottom number.
To convert 1/2 into a decimal, divide 1 by 2.
2 is bigger than one, so our answer is 0 r1

$$\frac{1}{2} \quad 1 \div 2 = 0.5$$

$$10 \div 2 = 5$$

Let's now take our remnant r1, pretend it's a 10, and divide it by 2. We got 5. Our decimal is 0.5
1/2 = 0.5

Now let's convert 1/4 into a decimal.
Divide 1 by 4. 4 is bigger than 1, so our answer is 0 r1.
Let's take our remnant r1, pretend it's a 10 and divide it by 4:
10 ÷ 4 = 2 r2
Pretend that our new remnant, r2 is 20 and divide it by 4 again: 20 ÷ 4 = 5
so 1/4 = 0.25

$$1 \div 4 = 0 \text{ R4}$$
$$\frac{1}{4} \quad 1 \div 4 = 0.25$$
$$10 \div 4 = 2 \text{ R2}$$
$$20 \div 4 = 5$$

Pretend that r2 is 20

Add and Subtract Your Decimals!

This is ridiculously easy. You can do it in your sleep (in class)!

1.351 + 2.5 = 3.851
zzzz....

All you need to do is write your decimals in a column, with the decimal points lined up.

```
  1.351
+ 2.5
-------
  3.851
```

That's all there is to it!

4.978 − 0.56 = 4.418

```
  4.978
− 0.56
-------
  4.418
```
Sweet dreams!!

Multiply Those Decimals!

Do you know how easy it is to multiply decimals? Even a pigeon can do this!

2.5 x 0.4 = ?

What will I get for that?

First, drop all the decimal points and zeros, and multiply your numbers:

25 x 4 = 100

Good! Now we put the decimal point in the answer. Where to put it?
Count how many digits are after the decimal point in the 2 numbers you are multiplying:
In 2.5 we have 1 digit after the decimal point
In 0.4 we have 1 digit after the decimal point
Total 2 digits.
So we count 2 digits from right to left in our answer and put the decimal point exactly there!
1.00

2.5 x 0.4 = 1.00 or just 1!

Let's do 0.03 x 1.2
3 x 12 = 36
In 0.03 and 1.2 there are a total of 3 digits after the decimal points.
Because 36 is less than 3 digits, we'll fill the empty spaces with zeros:
0.036
0.03 x 1.2 = 0.036

Boo! Have I scared you? **Relax!** Dividing decimals is not as scary as you think!

"I can get used to this."

$3.5 \div 0.7 = ?$

If both numbers have the same number of digits after the point, just drop the point and divide $35 \div 7 = 5$

If they have different numbers of digits after the point, like this: $4.34 \div 0.7 = ?$

1. Move the point in both numbers to the right by an equal number of digits, until your divisor's point is outside the number:

   4.34   43.4
   0.7   7.

2. Divide the portion before the point:
   $43 \div 7 = 6 \text{ r}1$
   So in your answer 6 will go before the point.

3. To find what comes after the point, ignore the point and divide $434 \div 7 = 62$
   So your answer is 6.2
   $4.34 \div 0.7 = 6.2$

Whose Room Is Bigger?

So 2 x 2 = 4, and we say 4 is the square of 2.
And look, it really is a square!

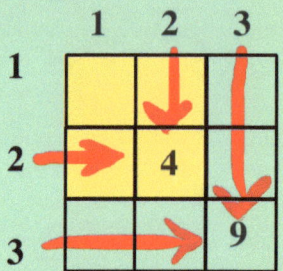

And 9 is the square of 3, because 3 x 3 = 9
This idea of the square is very useful, because this is how we measure the size of an area.
We measure area in various square units —
square inches, scuare feet, square centimeters, square meters, and so on.
So, for instance if I want to know how big my room is, here is how I will measure it in square meters.
I will measure the length of the room:
L = 3 meters
Then I will measure the width of the room:
W = 3 meters
Then I will multiply length by width:
L x W = 3 meters x 3 meters = 9 square meters
It's 9 square meters! That easy! Look:

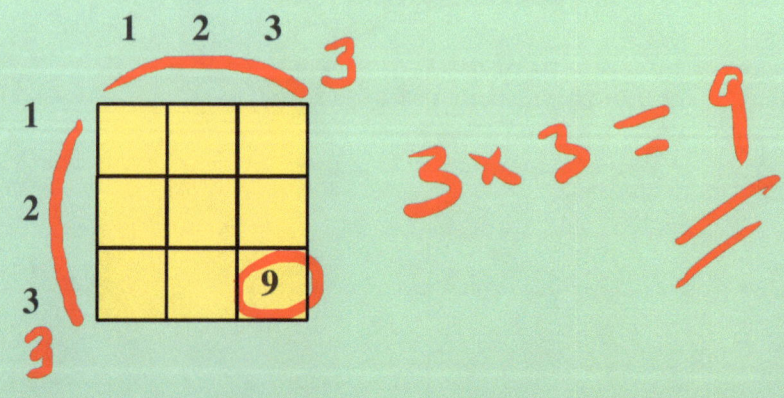

LOOK AT THESE KIDS.
WHY ARE THEY SCREAMING
AT EACH OTHER?
THE GIRL SAYS HER BROTHER'S
ROOM IS LARGER THAN HERS.
SHE WANTS HIS ROOM.
AND HE IS, LIKE, *NO WAY!*

WHAT TO DO?

LET'S MEASURE THEIR ROOMS
AND FIND OUT THE TRUTH!

HERE IS THE GIRL'S ROOM.
IT'S SQUARE. LET'S MEASURE IT:

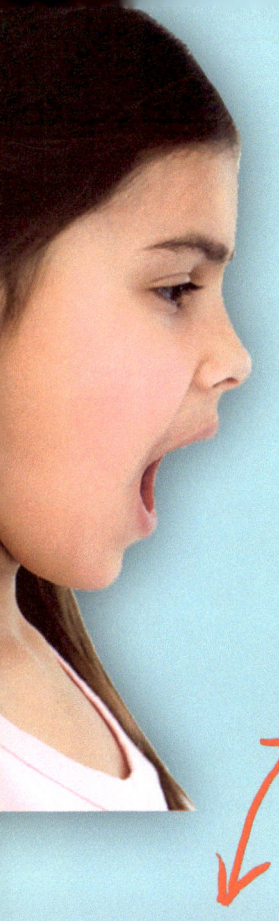

L = 5 METERS   W = 5 METERS
THE AREA OF HER ROOM IS
L x W = 5 x 5 = 25 SQUARE METERS

HERE IS HER BROTHER'S ROOM.
IT'S A RECTANGLE.
WE MEASURE RECTANGLE AREAS
THE SAME WAY AS SQUARE AREAS.

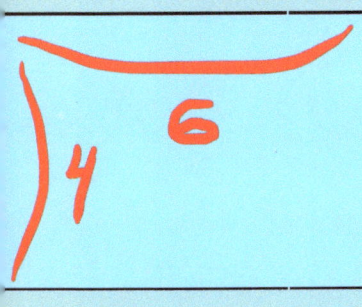

L = 6 METERS   W = 4 METERS
L x W = 6 x 4 = 24 SQUARE METERS

WOW! HIS ROOM IS ACTUALLY
SMALLER! IT'S LONGER SO MAYBE IT
JUST LOOKS BIGGER. HE SHOULD GO
AHEAD AND EXCHANGE IT FOR
HIS SISTER'S ROOM! HAHAHA!